Pros and Cons of Merit Pay

by
Susan Moore Johnson

Library of Congress Catalog Card Number 83-83085
ISBN 0-87367-203-8
Copyright © 1984 by the Phi Delta Kappa Educational Foundation
Bloomington, Indiana

This fastback is sponsored by the Wayne State University Chapter of Phi Delta Kappa, which made a generous contribution toward publications costs.

Table of Contents

Introduction	7
The Current Context for Merit Pay Proposals	9
How Merit Pay Works	12
Types of Merit Pay	12
Criteria for Awarding Merit Pay	14
Lessons of the Past	21
The Pros and Cons of Merit Pay	24
Arguments for Merit Pay	24
Arguments Against Merit Pay	25
Weighing the Arguments	28
The Experiences of Business and Government	29
Business	29
Government	31
Teachers as Workers and Schools as Workplaces	34
The Prospects for Merit Pay	37
References	41

Introduction

When President Reagan urged in May 1983 that teachers "be paid and promoted on the basis of their merit and competence," he voiced the public's wide dissatisfaction with its schools. His proposal for merit pay — a plan by which teachers' pay depends on the quality of their performance — was attractive for its logic, simplicity, and congruence with American values. Merit pay, its advocates argued, would encourage and reward effective instruction, edge poor teachers out of the classrooms, and ensure more efficient use of scarce dollars. The plan rapidly gained political and public support when it was promoted by several national education panels.

Many who worked in and worried about America's schools opposed the proposal, arguing that merit pay would be difficult to implement, would undermine morale, and would subject teachers to abuse and favoritism. Moreover, they said, merit pay had repeatedly failed in the past. But those who opposed merit pay could offer no alternative policy that promised improved performance and accountability for such a small investment.

A contentious debate between federal administrators and national union leaders followed. In the view of many, to resist merit pay was to resist reform and perpetuate mediocrity. As public support for merit pay grew, politicians from Washington to the states and local districts endorsed the notion. The U.S. House of Representatives Merit Pay Task Force concluded that "Despite mixed and inconclusive results with performance-based pay in the private sector and in education, we support and encourage experiments with performance-based pay." Florida legislators appropriated $80 million to implement a statewide merit pay plan in 1984-85. A number of other states considered merit pay plans in their school reform packages, and local school districts in many parts of the country studied and initiated a variety of plans that based teachers' pay on performance.

Those who seek to translate the seemingly straightforward principles of merit pay into practice will likely have many questions that remain unanswered by the political debate. What are the causal links between merit pay and better schools? What are the major arguments for and against merit pay? What can we learn from industry's experience with merit pay? What different forms might merit pay plans take, and are some more likely to work than others? What criteria can be used to distinguish one teacher's performance from another's? What can we learn from past merit pay initiatives? Would merit pay provide an effective incentive for good teaching? Would the policy have unintended consequences? Would it cost more or save money? These and other questions require careful consideration before school officials adopt merit pay policies.

In this fastback I shall examine the premises, practicalities, history, and politics of merit pay. First, I will describe the current context for performance-based pay proposals and explain how alternative plans work. Next, I will consider past efforts to institute merit pay in education and review the arguments for and against these plans. Since business and some parts of government have instituted merit pay plans, it is important to consider how they have worked and how they might be adapted to schools, given what we know about teachers as workers and schools as workplaces. Finally, I shall review the current prospects of merit pay for teachers and assess its worth as a schooling reform.

The Current Context for Merit Pay Proposals

In the current political debate about schooling, "merit pay" has become a catchword for teacher accountability and its meaning has been muddied. In this discussion, "merit pay" will refer to those policies that pay different wages to teachers who have the same job descriptions and work obligations. The differences in compensation, which may be one-time bonuses or permanent increases, are based on systematic assessments of performance. Merit pay plans should be distinguished from other incentive plans that pay teachers more for different kinds or amounts of work. For example, career ladder plans leading to the rank of master teacher are not merit pay plans even though they may require that teachers be judged meritorious to participate; such plans typically require supervisory and research responsibilities as well as longer work years. While it may be politically expedient to label a variety of reform proposals "merit pay," it is misleading to do so.

Proposals for merit pay are a response to concerns about the quality and effectiveness of public education. Many are based on persuasive data about the shortcomings of schools. For example, an estimated 23 million U.S. adults and 13% of our 17-year-olds are functionally illiterate. The quality of new teachers, as measured by standardized test scores, has decreased over the past decade; and there is strong evidence that the teaching profession is attracting and holding the less capable college graduates. Many parts of the country report teacher shortages in mathematics and science, yet half of the newly employed mathematics, science, and English teachers reportedly are not qualified to teach those subjects. American students spend fewer days in school and less time on homework than their counterparts in other countries. In an international comparison of 19 academic tests, American students never scored first or second and scored lowest on seven of the tests. The decline in SAT scores that began in 1963 parallels a reduction in requirements for the high school diploma.

The problems, which seem to be legion, have been documented by researchers and publicized in the reports of national education commissions and task forces. In most of these reports, the shortcomings of the schools are linked to the security of the country. For example, in *A Nation at Risk* the National Commission on Excellence in Education warns of "a rising tide of mediocrity that threatens our very future as a nation and a people." The Task Force of the Twentieth Century Fund concurs that the nation's public schools are in trouble and warns of a "threatened disaster" for the nation, adding that "By almost every measure — the commitment and competency of teachers, student test scores, truancy and dropout rates, crimes of violence — the performance of our schools falls far short of expectations." Even John Goodlad, whose study of schooling is the most comprehensive and current examination of U.S. education, begins *A Place Called School* (1983) with alarm:

> American schools are in trouble. In fact, the problems of schooling are of such crippling proportions that many schools may not survive. It is possible that our entire public education system is nearing collapse.

It is not within the scope of this discussion to examine and weigh such assertions. Rather, it is important to recognize the extent of the problems that current reforms are proposed to remedy. Although no merit pay advocates have promised that performance-based pay will resolve all these problems, merit pay has been singled out by many as the key to widespread education reform.

The logic of merit pay is based on a set of assumptions about what teachers want, how teachers work, and how schools function. The first assumption is that teachers prefer performance-based pay over a standard salary scale. In trying to explain why so few highly qualified college students study to be teachers and why the best teachers are likely to leave the profession, some analysts conclude that teachers are disenchanted with compensation systems that treat all teachers the same. As one merit pay advocate recently argued in an editorial in the *American School Board Journal* (September 1983):

> Imagine being an effective hardworking teacher condemned to receive exactly the same raise as the listless, barely adequate dolt down the hall. To anyone reared on tales of Henry Ford and Horatio Alger, this wrongheadedness is so glaring that merely seeing it officially sanctioned must be grounds for despair.

Such arguments assume that teachers are not working as hard as they might and that competitive pay would serve as an incentive both for performing better and for remaining in the profession.

Second, merit pay proposals assume that dissatisfied, unchallenged teachers are a significant part of today's school problems, and that a competitive approach to their work could ultimately improve student learning.

Merit pay critics challenge these causal links and argue that while competitive pay may be consistent with the tenets of free enterprise, there is no certainty that its use in schools would make teachers happier or schools better. In fact, many argue that merit pay would divide faculties, undermine morale, and ultimately make schools less effective rather than more.

How Merit Pay Works

Although there are many variations in local merit pay plans, most are similar in three respects. First, merit is used to determine only a part of the teacher's pay, with salary increments typically being added to a guaranteed base. Occasional plans permit school administrators to withhold or reduce a teacher's annual increment for unsatisfactory work, but the base salary remains intact.

Second, merit is usually only one factor used to determine salary increments. In most cases, years of service, earned degrees, or completed graduate courses continue to determine more of a teacher's annual increment than does any performance assessment.

Third, in virtually all merit pay plans, decisions about a teacher's worth are based on systematic performance appraisals. Teachers do not participate in confidential one-to-one negotiations about salary raises as many college faculty or industrial managers do. Rather, the process and criteria by which deserving teachers are identified are publicly specified, often having been established through collective bargaining. Typically, decisions are based on observations of classroom performance that culminate in written evaluations. In some cases, student test scores rather than performance appraisals determine the pay differentials.

Given these similarities, there is still wide variation in the types of merit pay plans that have been developed locally. The following discussion examines some of these alternative plans.

Types of Merit Pay

One type of merit pay plan includes multiple salary scales, which determine the salaries of teachers in different performance groups. For example, the school system in Ladue, Missouri, has three salary scales, each of which leads to a different maximum pay. Only teachers who are judged to be superior can advance to Schedule III and attain the highest level of pay offered by the district.

Alternatively, there are merit pay systems that grant varying salary increments to teachers with different performance assessments. For example, in Niskayuna Central School District in Schenectady, New York, 200 of 240 teachers received merit pay in 1983. The amounts of individual awards, which ranged from $1,000 to $2,000, were determined by building administrators who conducted individual evaluations.

Third, there are merit pay plans that permit teachers to move toward the top of the salary scale at an accelerated rate of more than one step per year. For example, in Glastonbury, Connecticut, teachers qualify for a double increment if they are judged to be outstanding and have "demonstrated professional effectiveness and growth," as well as having "made a significant contribution to the school, department, school system, or educational field."

Fourth, some school districts have merit pay plans specifically designed for experienced teachers at the top of the salary scale. These permit outstanding teachers to exceed the maximum salary step by specified amounts. For example, in the Pentucket Regional School District of West Newbury, Massachusetts, teachers who have reached the maximum step in the "Masters Degree/36 Hours" column may apply for placement on the "Master Teachers Scale." Candidates who are judged by their principals to have demonstrated "leadership which resulted in activities that significantly improved the educational process in the school" are paid beyond the regular scale.

In each of these plans, the additional pay that a teacher receives in any year becomes part of that individual's salary base and thus increases the teacher's salary in all subsequent years. Most plans, however, award one-time bonuses to teachers who demonstrate merit. Typically, the district gives a fixed number of awards each year. For example, the superintendent in Carlisle, Massachusetts, recognizes the outstanding performance of six teachers each year with honorary awards of $1,000. Amherst-Pelham Regional School District, also in Massachusetts, awards bonuses of $800 to 12 teachers "who consistently demonstrate excellence in providing instructional services to school district children and who make significant professional contributions, beyond those outlined in the teacher position description, which benefit school district children." There are, of course, many combinations and variations of these five basic approaches to merit pay.

Criteria for Awarding Merit Pay

Deciding how merit pay plans are structured is easy compared to deciding such questions as: What criteria will be used to identify outstanding teachers? Is merit pay restricted to a few or available to an unlimited number of teachers? Is a teacher's special status a temporary or permanent benefit? How will teachers be observed and evaluated? Each of these questions warrants careful consideration.

Performance Criteria. There are generally three criteria used to select outstanding teachers: teacher characteristics, teaching performance, and outcome measures such as test scores. The first, teachers' personal characteristics — appearance, demeanor, or speech — are rarely used today as decisive factors in merit appraisals; rather, measures of academic preparation play a major role in determining a teacher's position on the salary scale. Teachers were often assessed on the basis of personal characteristics during the early part of the century, but 80 years of research failed to demonstrate that these were meaningful variables; and most districts dropped them from their evaluation instruments.

The vast majority of merit pay plans use assessments of classroom performance to award merit increases. Evaluators conduct one or more in-class observations and assess such things as a teacher's command of subject matter, lesson preparation, relationships with children, classroom management, and success in individualizing instruction. Evaluation instruments also include non-instructional performance criteria — a teacher's professional growth (typically referring to inservice training or advanced coursework), relationships with colleagues, and contribution to the school as a whole.

Although performance evaluation instruments are remarkably similar from district to district, it is rare to find two that include exactly the same criteria. This variation reflects the lack of consensus among academics and practitioners about what makes for good teaching.

In the current quest for accountability, many education critics are demanding more attention to outcomes than to process. Therefore, an increasing number of merit pay plans reward teachers whose students progress beyond expectations, typically measured by their performance on standardized tests. For example, in the Weber School District in Ogden, Utah, teachers can qualify for a $1,300 bonus that is awarded on the basis of student achievement test scores. In Seiling, Oklahoma, teachers whose students test above projected levels also receive merit increments.

Recently, districts have begun to reward entire school staffs for schoolwide improvement of students' test scores, apparently in response to research findings about the importance of teachers' shared purpose in effective schools. For example, in addition to rewarding individual teachers for success in their classrooms, Seiling grants additional increments to all staff if their school's average student test scores exceed projections. A similar new program in Dallas, Texas, awards merit pay to all teachers in the top 25% of schools making "exceptional progress" as measured by student test scores. Computers track the performance of individual students and each school is compared to past student achievement trends and the achievement trends of similar students across the district.

None of the three sets of criteria that might be used to assess teachers' worth is without criticism. Teacher characteristics are widely thought to be weakly related to effective instruction. Relying on variables related more closely to instruction — preparation, classroom management, and discussion skills — is only somewhat less problematic because so little can be proven about effective instruction. Are lectures better than discussions? Is small group work better than whole class instruction? Should classrooms be structured and teacher-centered or open and student-centered? The "right" responses to these questions are more a function of educational and political fashion than conclusive research.

Given this uncertainty, it is not surprising that districts are increasingly seeking indicators of instructional outcomes to identify outstanding teachers. However, tests — the only comparative measure of instructional outcomes that is available — measure only part of what is taught in schools, and they probably are accurate only for some students. Tests do not assess creative expression or citizenship. Moreover, some students do not test well, while others test far beyond their routine performance.

Quotas. A second important question to be addressed in designing a merit pay plan is whether there should be a limit placed on the number of teachers eligible for recognition or whether there is unlimited opportunity for advancement. Each approach is used in some school districts, and there are arguments supporting both approaches.

By establishing a quota system in which merit pay awards are restricted to a specified number or percentage of teachers, a school district implicitly endorses a competitive policy. If merit pay is intended to promote excellence by rewarding teachers competitively, then logically it must reward them selectively. In the Clayton, Missouri, Public Schools a maximum of four awards of $5,000 each can be awarded to outstanding teachers. In the Le Roy Community Unit School District 2 in Illinois, a maximum of 20% of the teachers in each school can receive a $500 award, and another 10% can receive a $250 award.

Cost is a compelling reason for establishing quotas on merit pay awards. Although many advocates suggest that merit pay plans could save money or would not increase costs by simply redistributing the current salary allocation, experience proves otherwise. In a survey of merit pay plans (Calhoun and Protheroe, 1983), the Educational Research Service found that "based on the costs of each plan per *all* teachers in a district, the average cost of merit pay among responding districts was $207 per teacher." This does not include administrative costs. Obviously, if a district limits the number of merit pay recipients, it can better control the costs of the program.

However, there are problems associated with quotas. In order to be an effective incentive, merit pay must seem attainable. If awards are severely limited, teachers may not regard working for a merit increase as a realistic goal. Also, while quotas underscore the selectivity of merit pay awards, there are many who contend that the competition they promote is destructive. They argue that restricting the number of teachers who can attain meritorious status may encourage staff to work in isolation and to withhold help from others. Therefore, a number of school districts have instituted merit pay plans with unlimited opportunities for success. For example, in Perryton, Texas, there is no quota placed on the number of teachers who can earn merit pay. In 1983 approximately 62% of the staff received merit awards ranging from $100 to $2,600.

One way that districts limit the eligibility for merit pay without promoting distrust among staff is to require teachers to have taught a specified number of years before being considered for merit pay. For example, in Lower Merion, Pennsylvania, teachers can earn from "one to four incentive increments of six hundred dollars ($600) each for extraordinary performance," but they must have worked four years and earned six semester hours of graduate credit before becoming eligible for the first increment, and another four years before becoming eligible for the second.

Quotas emphasize the special status of teachers who earn merit pay and control the costs of the program. However, quotas also may discourage initiative among teachers who regard merit pay as an unattainable distinction, or they may promote bad feelings among teachers who see themselves in competition with other teachers for merit awards.

Temporary or Permanent Awards. A third question in designing a merit pay plan is whether the status achieved by teachers is temporary or permanent. In districts that award a small number of bonuses to a fixed number or percentage of teachers, the one-time awards do not affect subsequent salaries. However, in some cases such as the Lower Merion School District plan discussed above, the increments become part of the base salary. Plans that permit teachers to exceed the maximum salaries also confer benefits throughout the duration of a teacher's career. Permanent plans are obviously more costly but are likely to promote less anxiety and uncertainty than awards that are determined annually. However, once achieved, permanent plans are probably no more likely to serve as incentives for continued high performance than single salary scales. In such cases, merit pay may cease to distinguish among teachers and instead become an entitlement.

The Evaluation Process. The final issue — how the evaluation process should be structured — is in many ways the most critical and complex. Fears of unfair evaluations have interfered with the adoption of many merit pay plans, and charges of favoritism have forced the termination of many others. Therefore, the technical questions of who observes and evaluates teachers, how those evaluators are trained, how many observations they conduct, how the assessments are compiled and the awards distributed, and whether there is an appeal process are more than technicalities.

It is assumed that the same performance standards will apply district-wide and a teacher of outstanding performance in one school will be comparable to such a teacher in another school. However, because building principals rather than central office administrators are the observers and evaluators in most districts, reliability can become a serious problem. Principals may adhere to different standards for average or above-average performance. Moreover, many principals may be inexperienced evaluators, having evaluated teachers irregularly or not at all in the past. Evaluations that were once of little practical consequence now are used to determine wages; and school districts that institute merit pay must ensure that administrators are skilled in classroom observations and practiced in writing evaluations that discriminate among teachers' performances.

There are considerable costs associated with instituting a thorough, fair evaluation process. The time and expense of training administrators and ensuring the reliability of their ratings are often unanticipated. Moreover, the process of observing, conferring, and writing consumes a great deal of administrative time. The principal of an 18-teacher school who is obliged to conduct two observations annually with pre- and post-observation conferences, would spend a minimum of 54 hours in meetings and observations and another 36 hours preparing the written evaluations. A school official in Bloomingdale, Illinois, estimated that building administrators in that district spend more than 50% of their time on teacher evaluation. Merit evaluations are more likely to be fair and to gain teachers' support if they are based on multiple classroom observations or if they are conducted by multiple observers, which further increases the time and costs needed to implement the program. Clearly, there are trade-offs associated with such an allocation of time; curriculum development, parent outreach, and building management get less attention.

The merit pay plans of local districts designate different individuals or groups to decide who will receive merit pay and how much money will be awarded. In rare cases, both decisions are made by the principal. However, most merit pay plans provide for a central office administrator or committee to review the principals' written evaluations and recommendations and make final decisions. In the Dundee Community Unit School District in Illinois, for example, decisions are made by a central committee composed of six teachers and five administrators.

Since many local districts that adopt merit pay plans also bargain collectively with their teachers, evaluators must abide by the due process protections of teachers' contracts. These are generally guarantees of fair play; for example, that a teacher be notified in advance of a formal evaluation, be observed for a substantial length of time, and be given a copy of the written evaluation. However, some contracts include more exacting procedural requirements; for example, that the first evaluation must be completed by December 15th, that the post-evaluation conference must be held within 48 hours of the observation, or that teachers must be given specific, written recommendations for improving any deficiency. Few of the local merit pay plans described by the Educational Research Service include the right of appeal. However, it seems likely that in most districts where teachers are unionized, the procedural elements of the evaluation process will be subject to challenges through the grievance process, and the program will require even more standardization and supervision by central office administrators.

Several respondents to the Educational Research Service survey reported that the right to keep merit awards confidential was an important factor in making their plans work. The Westside Community Schools in Omaha, Nebraska, never publishes information about the recipients or size of its merit awards even though a large sum, $35,000, is spent on the incentive program. School officials in San Marino, California, also kept merit pay awards confidential; but reportedly, teachers in San Marino obtained a list of recipients as a matter of public record and distributed it. This provoked dissatisfaction among teachers who had not been judged meritorious, and the plan was dropped in 1983. In many school districts, particularly those with strong teacher unions, it seems unlikely that introducing confidential merit pay plans will be acceptable.

Instituting merit pay is a complicated process that involves conceiving a program that is consistent with the goals and practices of a district, convincing the staff that it is fair and worthy of their support, and maintaining it with administrative training. Questions such as who conducts the evaluations, whether the decisions can be appealed, and whether the names of the recipients are made public are important ones on which the success or failure of a program may rest.

Lessons of the Past

Merit pay gained sudden national attention in the spring of 1983, but it was not a new idea. Merit pay plans were popular during two prior periods of school reform marked by widespread concern about the international standing of the United States. After World War I school administrators across the country earnestly applied the principles of Frederick Taylor's Scientific Management to education and strived to make their schools more rigorous, efficient, and businesslike. Again during the late 1950s and early 1960s, after the Russians launched Sputnik, there were many curricular and administrative school reforms, including merit pay. The current national focus on schooling is also precipitated by concern for the country's international standing, this time its economic position relative to Japan and other industrialized countries. The demands for greater productivity, accountability, and performance-based pay are reminiscent of the past. A brief review of that past can help local policymakers proceed more realistically in the present.

In 1916 Ellwood P. Cubberley, perhaps the most influential educator at the time, decried the uniform salary schedule as a "poor use of funds" and urged an alternative system that would "pay the most to those deserving the most," while encouraging "personal growth on the part of all not hopelessly dead." He argued that the single salary scale "presupposes that all of the same rank and experience are approximately of equal worth — a condition that is never found." He concluded that a merit pay plan would:

> provide a much better distribution of rewards; would offer more encouragement for study and personal advancement; would provide more

opportunities for the efficient to rise; would tend better to retain the best teachers in the service; and would give the school directors better returns in efficiency for the money spent than does the present salary schedule.

In response to this and similar exhortations, local school boards instituted merit pay plans nationwide. By various estimates, between 18% and 48% of the country's school districts paid teachers by performance between 1918 and 1928. The plans in effect were varied: determining teachers' increments on the basis of their merit ratings, awarding different increases to different merit groups, and basing individuals' maximum attainable salaries on their performance ratings.

Between 1935 and 1955, these merit pay plans fell into disuse, and single salary schedules again prevailed. When merit pay was revived during the late 1950s, the plans instituted by local districts closely resembled those of the 1920s. However, they had been modernized. School officials in Summit, New Jersey, hired a management consulting firm to conduct a task analysis of teachers' work that would serve as the basis for evaluations. The Teacher Observation Code of the Weber School District in Ogden, Utah, required the evaluator to enter responses every five minutes during observations. And West Hartford, Connecticut, in an effort to "make final appraisal results independent of differences in rater discriminability," transformed each set of ratings into "a distribution with a predetermined common mean, standard deviation, and variance." The merit pay plans of the 1950s also included many standard features — annual ratings, multiple observers, and weighted criteria (Steffensen, 1962).

Though complex and refined, these merit pay plans did not prove to be very durable. During the 1960s approximately 10% of the country's local districts had merit pay in some form; by 1972 only 5.5% did. Moreover, an Educational Research Service study reported in 1979 found that half of the merit pay plans reported by districts had been in effect for no more than five years.

The question, of course, is why merit pay plans fail. There appears to be no simple answer. The Educational Research Service surveyed 239 local districts in 1979 and found that merit pay plans had been discontinued for a wide range of reasons — administrative, personnel, collective bargaining, and financial. Some districts abandoned the plans when teachers opposed them or administrators decided that they destroyed morale and caused dissension. Others were dropped because of difficulties in applying the criteria fairly when evaluating staff. Some local districts found that the plans did not improve teaching performance, while others decided that the purpose of their plans had been compromised when virtually all teachers received merit increases. Many plans were abandoned at the negotiating table, while some were discontinued when new administrators found them incompatible with their philosophies. The Educational Research Service's 1983 survey confirmed these findings.

The responses of these districts suggest that merit pay is a fragile policy requiring careful planning and tending. Its purposes and procedures must be explicit and must be shared by teachers and administrators. If the criteria for merit are based on classroom performance, administrators must be well trained in observing and evaluating teachers and have sufficient time to observe, confer, and prepare written evaluations. To win teacher acceptance, merit pay plans must be securely financed, with performance-based increases added to competitive salaries. Strong administrative commitment also seems to be a key factor in their survival. Two of the longest lasting performance-based pay plans, in Ladue, Missouri, and San Marino, California, were administered throughout their duration by superintendents who resolutely supported the principles of merit pay.

The experiences of these districts provide lessons for today's policymakers. The wisdom of merit pay is not self-evident; its procedures are not self-perpetuating; its survival is not assured.

The Pros and Cons of Merit Pay

Because merit pay proposals are based on an untested set of causal assumptions about teachers and schooling, many of the arguments for and against merit pay are unproven assertions about its likely effects. The following summary of these arguments will familiarize readers with the points of the debate.

Arguments for Merit Pay

Merit Pay is consistent with the tenets of free enterprise. Teachers, like other individuals in our society, should have the opportunity to achieve to their highest potential and to be rewarded for their accomplishments. The single salary scale, which is used by most local districts, rewards teachers for their graduate coursework and longevity, but not for their effectiveness as instructors. Performance-based pay systems would identify teachers who achieve outstanding success in their work and compensate them for their extra effort and productivity. Teachers who do not excel would be indirectly penalized by receiving only their base salaries. Advocates of merit pay regard this as a just distribution of rewards.

Merit pay would keep better teachers in education while dissuading ineffective teachers from remaining. By recognizing and rewarding outstanding teaching, merit pay would increase the likelihood that good teachers would feel appreciated. Moreover, the opportunity to earn additional income would serve as an incentive to remain in teaching. This argument acknowledges that teachers' status and salaries are not competitive with status and salaries in other professions. It assumes that the best teachers leave the profession, in part, because of low recognition or pay. If they were singled out and rewarded for their accomplishments, they would be more likely to remain in teaching.

Merit pay would stimulate teachers to be critical of their own work and would promote healthy competition. Teacher tenure and the single salary scale guarantee security but do not promote teachers' ongoing assessment of their work. A teacher who achieves tenure could be using the same lesson plans 30 years later, yet each year would receive the same raise as colleagues who regularly improve their teaching. The opportunity to win merit increases would encourage teachers to improve their performance. Because teachers would be aware that competitive pay systems reward only selected teachers, they would be attentive to the accomplishments of their colleagues and would themselves strive to excel.

Taxpayers would more willingly support public education if teachers were paid according to their performance. The public is regularly confronted with evidence of the schools' failings — declining test scores, vandalism and violence, and declining teacher qualifications. Yet school costs continue to rise, often as enrollments decline. When taxpayers are asked to support school levies, they often argue that they are being asked to pay more for mediocre, unsatisfactory services. As the Gallup Poll indicates, the public believes that one of the basic problems of schooling is the low quality of teachers. If merit pay were instituted and teachers were paid for what they produce, citizens might more readily accept tax increases. More rigorous efforts by educators to increase productivity, and thus to demonstrate that they are frugal with the tax dollar, would be rewarded by increased public support.

Arguments Against Merit Pay

There is no agreement about what good teaching is or how to measure it. Despite many years of research, educators have not determined what constitutes effective teaching. Studies of teacher characteristics have revealed few correlates of effective instruction. Of all the characteristics studied, verbal ability alone appears to be significantly related to student outcomes, a finding that many regard as self-evident. Nor have studies of instructional techniques yielded more definitive answers. While all teachers must be able to do certain things — plan lessons, keep order, maintain momentum, ask questions, monitor student progress — debate persists about the best way to do these things. Moreover, it is the administrator's judgment rather than some unerring gauge that measures a teacher's effectiveness. Until objective measures of teaching effectiveness are available, pay differentials cannot truly be performance-based.

The evaluation system that supports most merit pay plans is inherently unreliable and potentially inequitable. Teachers working in different buildings and being evaluated by different administrators often compete for a limited number of merit pay awards. Because the principals in various schools inevitably have different expectations and values, teachers are assessed by different standards. Some evaluators are tougher than others; some stress discipline, others emphasize discovery learning. A teacher judged to be outstanding by one principal might be considered deficient by another. Because written evaluations may not be comparable from school to school, it would be difficult to award merit pay competitively.

Because teacher evaluations are subjective, their substance seldom can be refuted. Few evaluation forms in use require specific data to substantiate either positive or negative judgments. Believing that favoritism and patronage are common in public education, teachers who oppose merit pay warn about its potential for administrative abuse and argue that although single salary scales may not reward outstanding teachers, they also cannot be manipulated.

Merit pay plans would interfere with effective supervision and encourage conformity rather than growth. Effective supervision provides a structured opportunity for administrators to improve instruction. However, for the process to work effectively, teachers must be candid about their problems, open to criticism, and ready to take risks and make changes. This is possible in non-threatening contexts; but when teachers are being judged and paid competitively on the basis of classroom observations, the professional growth benefits of supervision are lost. Teachers become more cautious about revealing their weaknesses and are more reluctant to change. Instead, teachers search for their evaluators' particular preferences and conform to them. In some cases, this conformity might improve teaching; but it might simply perpetuate poor performance.

Merit pay plans are not cost effective. One of the greatest attractions of merit pay is the promise that there will be major gains on a small investment. In fact, many believe that merit pay might actually save money by redistributing the current salaries of teachers. However, there is evidence that incentive pay plans increase salary costs with no guarantee of instructional improvement. In addition, there are substantial administrative costs associated with merit pay if it is to be instituted responsibly. Administrators must be trained to observe and evaluate staff, which costs both time and money. They must spend considerable time on classroom observations and teacher conferences. The time spent administering a merit pay plan means time lost to curriculum development or inservice training. The costs may not be worth the investment.

Competitive pay undermines teacher morale and compromises collegiality. Merit pay plans are potentially destructive. If teachers are competing for scarce rewards, they will be less trusting and less likely to share their ideas and materials with colleagues. In schools where teachers disagree with the evaluative criteria or distrust evaluators, cynicism and bitterness may prevail. Cooperation and a sense of shared purpose among staff are important in making a school work well; and if merit pay incentives encourage teachers to work on their own behalf rather than on behalf of the whole school, students of exemplary teachers may profit at the expense of students in other classrooms. The quality of curriculum development, building supervision, and inservice training may all be diminished by merit pay plans that stress the accomplishments of the individual over the accomplishments of the group.

Merit pay rewards a few teachers but does not raise the general level of teaching. There is no evidence that merit pay will ultimately improve schools. It is assumed that all teachers will be motivated to work for merit increases; but, even if they do, it may be that no teacher's performance will be substantially improved. Rather, the outstanding teachers will continue to succeed as they always have; and the average or below average teachers, who regard merit pay as unattainable, may even reduce their efforts in discouragement. If the problems of the teaching profession are as serious and pervasive as the critics and commission studies conclude, then a systematic, thorough approach to improving teaching is necessary, one that directly addresses the problems of average and poor teachers. Merit pay is not such an approach. Identifying good teaching may be an important element of efforts to improve the profession, but it is insufficient in itself and may prove to be counterproductive.

Weighing the Arguments

Most of the arguments for and against merit pay are based on assumptions about how teachers will respond and beliefs about how to improve instruction. Those who advocate merit pay think that the prospect of salary increases will motivate teachers to work harder, and that their efforts will improve student learning. Merit pay opponents base their arguments on a different set of assumptions. They contend that differential pay will more likely demoralize than inspire teachers because accurate assessments of teaching performance are impossible. While advocates center their hopes on individual achievements, opponents look at the group and conclude that merit pay might reduce the overall effectiveness of the teaching staff.

In weighing the validity of these contradictory beliefs about performance-based pay, it is useful to consider the use and efficacy of merit pay in other settings. The experiences of business and government provide instructive examples, which are discussed in the next chapter.

The Experiences of Business and Government

Those who urge that teachers be paid by performance often contend that because merit pay works in other professions, it should work in education. The following discussion first reviews the use of merit pay in business and industry and then the experiences of various levels of government in adapting merit pay principles to the public sector.

Business

The premises and practices of merit pay would seem to be compatible with those of the pragmatic world of business. The opportunity for individual initiative and achievement, the ongoing assessment of productivity, and faith in competition's salutary effects would all seem to enhance the prospects of merit pay. However, Edward E. Lawler, an expert on compensation and motivation, reports in *Pay and Organization Development* that "the principle of paying for performance is often honored more in the breach than in reality." Merit pay is not nearly as common in the private sector as many believe.

Lawler reports that merit pay is an effective incentive in some parts or types of business, but not others. For example, in sales or piecework, where the sum of many individuals' competitive efforts increases the productivity of the entire company, merit pay can be an effective incentive. In this case, employees' individual productivity can be readily compared by a count of widgets made or sold. Because employees work independently, they do not interfere with each others' efforts. Lawler observes that in such settings it is "appropriate to implement an incentive plan that motivates these employees to maximize their individual productivity and to pay little attention to cooperative activities."

However, much of business is neither sales nor piecework. Rather, many businesses and parts of businesses depend on the coordinated efforts of many employees. Lawler observes that merit pay is inappropriate for work that must be done "either successively (work that passes from one person to another, e.g., assembly operations) or coordinately (work that is a function of the joint effort of all employees, e.g., process production as is done in chemical plants)."

On reflection, one realizes that there are very few work situations where an individual's contribution can be isolated and assessed. For example, in designing the marketing plan for a new product, employees' work is both interdependent and interactive. Not only would it be difficult to assess accurately each individual's performance, but doing so might inhibit employees' cooperation and compromise their creative efforts. Only if all members of the group benefit from the success of their product will they contribute freely and cooperatively to the process.

Because so much work in business and industry is complex, many of the merit pay plans that do exist measure group performance rather than individual performance. When incentive payments are based on the performance of a division or entire plant, individuals recognize that it is in their self-interest to work together so that the whole organization functions well. However, one weakness of group merit pay plans is that individuals' pay and performance are not tightly linked. Employees may not see how their own work contributes to the overall effectiveness of their group and, therefore, may not be motivated by the pay incentive.

Business, like education, has difficulty with identifying the criteria of effective performance. Although one can readily measure objects produced, sales made, or dollars earned, it is not clear how to assess objectively the work of designers, buyers, or supervisors. Where subjective criteria are applied, issues of trust and rater reliability surface, just as they do in education.

It is interesting to note that although merit pay is consistent with traditional American business values — employee independence and self-sufficiency, competition, and specialization — many successful American companies such as IBM, Hewlett-Packard, and Intel promote employee interdependence and minimize pay differentials or gear their performance-based pay toward groups rather than individuals.

Government

In business and industry a competitive economy can theoretically regulate pay incentives as production costs and consumer choice provide the standards of success for a product or service. However, in the public sector there is no such objective standard. Administering merit pay in agencies and services such as libraries, police forces, or public housing authorities can be very complicated. Yet there have been a number of recent efforts by various levels of government to increase productivity with pay incentives.

The largest public-sector merit pay effort was initiated by the Civil Service Reform Act of 1978, which mandated that the pay of Civil Service grades 13-15 for supervisors and management officials be based on their performance ratings. One requirement of that merit pay plan — that its cost not exceed that of the previous system — necessarily limited the number and size of merit increases.

There have been a number of problems identified with that performance-based pay plan. Jone L. Pearce and James L. Perry (1981) found that employees did not believe that their performance was being accurately measured and were not motivated by the prospect of higher pay for better performance. Participants in the study reported that although they were willing to work harder for additional pay, they did not regard the criteria being used as "the best ones to promote improved performance or agency effectiveness."

Three additional findings from this study are worth noting. First, these managerial employees did not regard pay as the most important reward in their work. In fact, when they were asked to rate the various rewards available to them, they repeatedly ranked "challenging work responsibilities" and "retirement benefits" first and second, respectively. Pay, which was ranked fifth in June 1980 before the plan began, temporarily moved to third place, but returned to fifth place by December 1981. This shift suggests that merit pay only temporarily served as an incentive for improved performance.

Second, the imposition of quotas within pay pools and the right of merit pool managers to change performance ratings undermined the credibility of the system and bred dissatisfaction among the managerial employees. These two factors diminished employees' confidence that pay differentials would actually be based on performance. Pearce and Perry probably voiced the doubts of many they surveyed when they asked, "If the ratings are accurate, why should they be manipulated?"

Third, the researchers reported that there was widespread "gaming" or goal displacement among employees who became less concerned with effective management and more attentive to getting good scores. Pearce and Perry report:

> There is clear evidence that the setting of these specific standards has focused managerial actions on their attainment; managers work hard to obtain good ratings on those standards that are measured. Yet not all of those actions could be considered "good management."

While one might legitimately argue that there is merit pay in the Civil Service, the various problems encountered with employee dissatisfaction, quotas, and manipulated ratings suggest that the program is not an unqualified success.

In addition to this large federal merit pay initiative, state and local governments have established various performance-pay plans. John M. Greiner and his associates at the Urban Institute published a comprehensive study of such efforts in 1981. They found that merit pay was the most common type of monetary incentive being used, but that its effectiveness was limited by a number of problems — the absence of objective criteria focused on job performance, the lack of flexibility in the rewards available for outstanding performance, the difficulty (or impossibility) of rewarding employees who had reached the top step of their salary range, competition for the same funds between cost-of-living increases and performance increases, and managers' resistance to completing personnel evaluations. "As a result," they conclude, "there has often been little reward for 'merit' under merit pay systems." They found that individualized merit pay awards often generated intense employee opposition, while group incentives were more acceptable. They argue that objective performance criteria can be defined more accurately for a group than for an individual.

These reports on merit pay from business and government provide important lessons for educators who seek to institute merit pay. First, employees may be more motivated by challenging work responsibilities or fringe benefits than opportunities for competitive pay. Second, it is important that the evaluated criteria of a merit pay plan reflect the most important elements of employees' work so that they will direct their efforts toward the right goals rather than just measurable goals. Third, individualized merit pay is appropriate for some kinds of work and not others. Competition among employees may be counter-productive in work that is sequential or that requires cooperation. Fourth, individuals are motivated by merit pay only to the extent that they believe extra effort will be rewarded. The more subjective merit ratings are, the more likely employees will decide that they are not worth working for.

Teachers as Workers and Schools as Workplaces

Schools are not businesses, and teachers have different roles and responsibilities than bureaucrats. Although much can be learned from experiences with merit pay in the private sector and government, it is important to consider what is unique about schools, teachers, and teaching before assessing the appropriateness of merit pay in education.

Unlike business and industry, where a company's objectives can be specified and its effectiveness in meeting them assessed, the goals and outcomes of schooling are often unspecified and unmeasurable. Standardized test scores, the most objective measure of student achievement, can be used to assess only some of schooling's goals. Multiple choice tests can tell little about students' progress in creative expression, artistic appreciation, citizenship, logic, inquiry skills, or moral reasoning.

The components of effective teaching are similarly hard to define. Researchers have failed to identify the characteristics of effective teachers or effective teaching. What is clear is that there are many different styles of good teaching and that it is difficult to separate teaching expertise from the individual. Although welders and salesmen undoubtedly encounter uncertainty and exercise discretion in their work, they do know what success is — a good weld, a final sale — and they know when they have achieved it. This is not always true with teachers.

If the product of schooling is a well-educated student, individual teachers control only a piece of that product. However, performance-based pay plans assess each year of the teacher's work as if it were the entire production process or as if the pieces of that process were simply additive. Teachers can neither control the quality or preparedness of the students they teach, nor can they accurately predict or regulate the uneven developmental rates of student learning. A second-grade teacher's success in laying the groundwork of mathematical reasoning may not become apparent until her students reach the fifth grade; the chance that the teacher will then be credited with the success is slim. Conversely, students who perform satisfactorily in first-year French may begin to fall behind in the second year because they never really learned the irregular verbs in the introductory course. Test scores will never reveal the source of the problem. For these reasons, teachers recognize that their work is interdependent, though often isolated. As individuals, they can influence, but not control the outcome.

Although education research has not been very effective in identifying the characteristics of effective teachers, we are beginning to understand some things about effective schools. In their review of the literature on effective schools, Stewart Purkey and Marshall Smith (1983) note the importance of a school culture that is "conducive to teaching and learning" and is achieved by "building staff agreement on and commitment to clearly and commonly identified norms and goals." Similarly, Judith Warren Little (1981) has found that efforts to change schools are more effective when teachers share common goals and promote collegiality and cooperation.

We have also learned some things about teachers as a social group. In general, teachers are conservative and more concerned with financial security than entrepreneurial opportunities. Most teachers do not enter teaching because of the pay. Rather, they look forward to a steady, moderate income and to work that is inherently rewarding. Recently, John Goodlad and his associates questioned more than 1,300 teachers and found that the majority entered teaching because of the nature of the work itself. Those who quit did so out of personal frustration and dissatisfaction with their teaching situation. Money, which had not been a major reason for entering teaching, ranked second in importance as a reason for leaving. Apparently, when teachers became disappointed with their work, pay took on more importance.

For merit pay to motivate workers toward organizational goals, it must be compatible with the character of the work, the structure of the workplace, and the priorities of the workers. An ideal setting for merit pay would be a piecework factory where objective appraisals are possible, cooperation among workers is unnecessary, and individuals are motivated by the opportunity to earn more money. But teaching is more akin to a production line than piecework. Good schools require that teachers acknowledge their interdependence and work cooperatively rather than compete.

The Prospects for Merit Pay

A number of factors increase the likelihood that many school districts will adopt merit pay plans in the next several years. First, there is widespread political pressure for greater accountability in schools. From the U.S. Department of Education to local school boards across the country, elected and appointed officials are insisting that new funds for education be tied to differential rewards for teachers. Some local officials, persuaded by such arguments, will devise new ways of adapting merit pay to public schools. Other districts will adopt small merit pay bonus plans as symbolic gestures to their communities.

However, there is not only political pressure for merit pay from outside the schools, there is growing support from within. Both teachers and union leaders have moderated their opposition to merit pay. Marilee C. Rist reported in the September 1983 *American School Board Journal* that "A clear majority — 62.7 percent — of teachers responding [to a nationwide poll] agree that teachers should be paid according to how well they perform in the classroom." Leaders of the American Federation of Teachers and the National Education Association have begun to acknowledge the political necessity of accommodating to the demands for merit recognition, although they have continued to oppose competitive merit pay plans that would single out individual teachers.

Despite the growing interest among educators in proposals for career ladders, it seems unlikely that they will replace merit pay proposals in most reform packages, largely because they are expensive and even more administratively complex than merit pay programs. A career ladder requires the development of a complicated evaluation system, extensive administrative training, and considerable funds to support substantially higher salaries for participating teachers. By contrast, merit pay seems simple and cheap. Bonus plans that identify a few outstanding teachers each year probably will not generate the opposition from staff that a fundamental reshaping of the single salary schedule would.

Assuming that merit pay will be adopted by many school districts over the next few years, what are its long-term prospects for reforming education? Will it provide incentive for improving teaching, as many argue? I conclude that it will not provide that incentive, and that the money, time, and spirit spent trying to make merit pay work would be better spent elsewhere.

Merit pay proposals assume that if teachers are given the chance to earn performance-based increases, they will work harder. This is unsupported by what we know about teachers and their work. Teachers' widespread dissatisfaction with their pay centers on low salaries rather than on the absence of competitive opportunities. Strong egalitarian norms among teachers would likely counteract their willingness to compete for the small pay differentials included in most merit pay plans.

Compounding the issue is the difficulty of convincing teachers that merit increases are actually determined by performance. Many research studies have shown that one of the most important factors in the effectiveness of performance-based pay is the extent to which pay is explicitly dependent on performance. But that is extremely difficult to ensure. Performance criteria are hard to define and measure, and the evaluation process is subject to misuse and abuse. Teachers are likely to be skeptical that their increased efforts or successes will be either recorded or rewarded.

In addition to eliciting more work from teachers, merit pay plans are intended to encourage the best teachers to remain in teaching. However, John Goodlad's research indicates that teachers quit the profession primarily because they fail to achieve what they had hoped to achieve in their work. This finding suggests that dollars expended on reform efforts might be better directed toward improving teachers' working conditions — safety and order, books and materials, inservice training — than providing bonuses to selected staff. To the extent that the best teachers leave their work because of low pay, substantial salary increases rather than symbolic bonuses would probably be necessary to retain them.

Third, and most important, merit pay is expected to improve instruction. However, the anticipated causal links between monetary incentives for teachers and instructional outcomes for students seem particularly weak. We have not yet determined how to improve instruction. If teachers respond to merit pay incentives, they will likely direct their energies toward those things that their evaluators regard as important. Sometimes those may lead to better learning; often they will not. Merit pay is not likely to motivate teachers or to improve instruction.

But there is a further problem — the unintended consequence of poor morale and discord. When the Educational Research Service asked local school districts with merit pay plans about the problems they encountered, a number of school officials pointed to problems among staff — jealousy, "disappointment and dissension," and "negative effect on staff morale." There are several sources of such problems. First, teachers who do not receive merit increases feel discouraged and unappreciated. Second, teachers may become demoralized by what they believe to be inappropriate criteria, inaccurate assessments, or inequitable procedures. Third, competition among staff for limited rewards may encourage isolation, selfishness, and anxiety. There is a fine line between healthy and unhealthy competition.

In order to function effectively, schools must be coherent organizations in which teachers recognize their interdependence and work together for shared purposes. There is much that already works against that coherence — isolated classrooms, age-graded instruction, seven-period days. There seems to be nothing in merit pay for individuals that would promote staff cooperation, and much that might further undermine it.

For these reasons, there have been some recent efforts to institute merit pay with group incentives. According to these plans, all teachers in schools where students make outstanding progress would receive merit bonuses. These plans may prove to encourage staff to work toward common goals, even though those goals may be somewhat limited by the test scores used to assess them. These are, at least in principle, more appropriate and promising adaptations of performance-based pay that recognize the realities of schools.

Throughout the debate about school reform, it is important to acknowledge that no single remedy will revive public education. Even the most skillfully designed and executed merit pay plan will not begin to resolve the current problems of lack of excellence, lack of equity, and financial deficits. Merit pay plans may have modest positive effects on the effort and career choices of some teachers, and they may appease the public. However, in deciding whether merit pay deserves their support, local school officials must weigh these anticipated benefits against substantial costs to the taxpayer and to the school as an organization.

References

Calhoun, Frederick S., and Protheroe, Nancy J. *Merit Pay for Teachers: Status and Descriptions.* Arlington, Va.: Educational Research Service, 1983.

Cubberly, Ellwood P. *The Portland Survey: A Textbook on City School Administration Based on a Concrete Study.* Yonkers on Hudson, N.Y.: World Book Company, 1916.

Goodlad, John I. *A Place Called School: Prospects for the Future.* New York: McGraw-Hill, 1983.

Greiner, John M., et al. *Productivity and Motivation: A Review of State and Local Government Initiatives.* Washington, D.C.: The Urban Institute, January 1981.

Lawler, Edward F. *Pay and Organization Development.* Reading, Mass.: Addison-Wesley Publishing Co., 1981.

Little, Judith Warren. "School Success and Staff Development: The Role of Staff Development in Urban Desegregated Schools." Mimeographed. Boulder, Colo.: Center for Action Research, January 1981.

Pearce, Jone L., and Perry, James L. "Federal Merit Pay: A Longitudinal Analysis." *Public Administration Review* 43 (July/August 1983): 315-25.

Porwoll, Paul J. *Merit Pay for Teachers.* Arlington, Va.: Educational Research Service, 1979.

Purkey, Stewart C., and Smith, Marshall S. "Educational Policy and School Effectiveness." Mimeographed. Madison: Wisconsin Center for Education Research, October 1983.

Rist, Marilee C. "Our Nationwide Poll: Most Teachers Endorse the Merit Pay Concept." *The American School Board Journal* 9 (September 1983).

Steffensen, James P. *Merit Salary Programs in Six Selected School Districts.* U.S. Department of Health, Education and Welfare Bulletin 1963, number 5. Washington, D.C., 1962.

```
331      Johnson, Susan Moore.
.2041       Pros and cons of
3711     merit pay.
J69
```

Ministry of Education, Ontario
Information Centre, 13th Floor,
Mowat Block, Queen's Park,
Toronto, Ont.   M7A 1L2